T0006925

ALSO BY RICHIE HOFMANN

Second Empire

A HUNDRED LOVERS

A HUNDRED LOVERS

Poems

RICHIE HOFMANN

ALFRED A. KNOPF, NEW YORK, 2024

THIS IS A BORZOI BOOK
PUBLISHED BY ALFRED A. KNOPF

Copyright © 2022 by Richie Hofmann

All rights reserved.
Published in the United States by Alfred A. Knopf,
a division of Penguin Random House LLC, New York, and distributed
in Canada by Penguin Random House Canada Limited, Toronto.
Originally published in hardcover in the United States by Alfred A. Knopf,
a division of Penguin Random House LLC, in 2022.

www.aaknopf.com

Knopf, Borzoi Books, and the colophon
are registered trademarks of Penguin Random House LLC.

Library of Congress Cataloging-in-Publication Data
Names: Hofmann, Richie, 1987– author.
Title: A hundred lovers: poems / Richie Hofmann.
Description: First edition. | New York: Alfred A. Knopf, 2022. |
"This is a Borzoi Book"—Title page verso.
Identifiers: LCCN 2021017895 (print) | LCCN 2021017896 (ebook) |
ISBN 9780593320983 (hardcover) | ISBN 9780593320990 (ebook) |
ISBN 9781524712051 (trade pbk)
Subjects: LCGFT: Poetry.
Classification: LCC PS3608.O4798 H86 2022 (print) |
LCC PS3608.O4798 (ebook) | DDC 811/.6—dc23
LC record available at https://lccn.loc.gov/2021017895
LC ebook record available at https://lccn.loc.gov/2021017896

Cover image: Greek marble statue c. 450 B.C.,
Museo Liebieghaus, Frankfurt. Album/Alamy
Cover design by Chip Kidd

Manufactured in Canada

Published February 8, 2022
First Paperback Edition May 28, 2024

CONTENTS

A HUNDRED LOVERS

Coquelicot

I pretend to sleep when he leaves.
He rubs his thumb across my chapped lips,
he touches the hair grown long around my ears.
I remember smelling him and the garrigue.
I leave by fast train, passing through suburbs,
poverty, dilapidated buildings so close
to destruction from within, poppies in full sun,
the blurring dross, the violet
graffiti, then nothing. My dirty clothes
packed above me, the T-shirt that carries his smell,
the weak black pepper of him,
the T-shirt he wiped his penis with.
I'm afraid of falling asleep,
because I will desire him in my sleep.

Every Night

I listened to the études through the early winter,
so quiet, so fine
even my breath could ruin them.
I asked my boyfriend to suffocate me,
I made him lick the mirror.
The nineteenth-century moldings
expressed an indifferent perfection. Breeze
at the window, our skins shivery.
I ate all the time at that place where they cut pizza with scissors
and you pay by the weight.
I kissed my classmates,
I walked aroused under the chestnuts.
Every night I told him
you should take a shower before you come over.

Street of Dyers

Coming home early in the morning,
I heard withered cats

behind the sycamores, the canal rushing
from a different century. The alleys

so quiet in this city I never really liked.
The widow with an Hermès scarf tied around her head

walked her ugly-beautiful dogs.
I lived behind a Louis XV door

in a room that imprisoned winter
even as spring was rife outside—

I was not in love, there was nothing to experience.

German Cities

Next week he will be away, auditioning:
Stuttgart. Frankfurt. Hamburg. Berlin.
We talk about music, style, discipline,
the great composers—
He sings and speaks
with the voice of a priest, father, or devil.
I pull on my jeans, in my pocket
the department store strip of paper
sprayed with cologne.
The garden that enters
the room is the garden of a childhood
in Munich; the naked old men
who smoked along the banks of the river
are dead now. My pocket smells of masculine lavender.

One Another

We are knotted in the white bedding.
I don't want sleep to separate us. We breathe
with the darkness, like an enormous animal.
Our bodies manufacture their odors. I taste earth
on his skin. Eros enters, where shame had lived.
Pale sun, then morning. How easily the earth closes
its cavities. I leave the apartment
wearing his black anorak.

Underground

My friend paid a little money.
We waited outside, above the stifling staircase.
A muscled boy danced foolishly.
Music pulsed through a window.
A $400 puppy mask,
light on our foreheads, the glasses sweating. His husband off
to the toilets to snort cocaine.
The room was full of shapes.
I wanted to feel tenderness,
but the love everyone was seeking
I already owned. All Sunday,
I was like a baby with a long memory
not able to touch or kiss anyone,
in the long twin bed with the lace coverlet.

At the Rustic Hamlet Built in 1783 for Marie Antoinette, Last Queen of France

No tourists.
Water turning a mill wheel,
    serving nothing but artifice.

    I am a servant
to order and erotic love.
    Soon to be

    yours.
You take a picture
    of me by a trellis,

    both of us failing
at the vernacular style.
    In the Temple of the God

    of Love, a naked
boy clutches an arrow.
    Once, in the manicured

    pasture, they reclined
holding shepherds' crooks,
    noble women

    who pretended
to be someone else,
    their wigless hair

tucked into
washed linen, their dresses
fastened with ribbons,

even now, the murdered queen
and her reassembled effects
making room

for art. We throw out
pieces of an unwanted
bâtard,

your gloved hand
feeding the pond—
the regal, monogamous

swan, the hungry,
whiskered fish
you drop the bread on.

Spring Wedding

The day before we married, we napped
in the afternoon, with no sheets over us,
and felt the breeze from the lake
on our backs and butts and legs. It felt different, a small
rebellion, though we've slept
in one another's arms for ten years,
like little beasts, vulnerable
and hairy, with saliva on our skin.
                                The next day
we were men again: ironed shirts, knotted
ties of silk, deodorant, parted hair, promises:
We will have children.
We will buy another house.
One of us will get cancer.
All of our parents will die.

Historic District

                    With purpose,
you pull up the blinds.
Light enters the room
like a feeling
violating a man.
Sitting up in a bed built for a husband
and a wife, I think for a second
nature has taken us back,
leaves scalloping
the plaster walls,
the ceiling.

The Toilet of Venus

The pages still uncut,
a book from the '40s
about Watteau—He gave it to me in the garden,
pulling it out of his tote bag.
We didn't kiss. The bugs were biting us.
All I wanted was to look at the paintings
—everyone swirling, a little ridiculous
in their extravagance, so many couples
or soon-to-be couples.
I don't know how
to explain my love of pleasure
without sounding like a creep.
When he saw me naked,
he said, You look like a grown-up Cupid.

Pink Room

We are contemporaries, born in
the worst plague year for our kind.
It is May, locust shells in the screen doors.
The surf is thick with ash. An unnamed man
roams the beach, looking for a place
deep inside himself, like a room lined in silk.
You're disgusting just like me.
Between us, three ceramic teeth
glued to our jaws. I leave my hair curly
for seven months. I love you because you can't be destroyed by love;
we are immune
to one another: my off-the-cuff Tennyson, your fingers
tearing the metal strings of a guitar. We stop
wearing underwear, spring lays its dust over everything.

Edible Flowers

We fill duffel bags with ripe fruit,
tearing off leaves that feel like human ears.
We put flowers in our mouths,
the two of us whose bodies have no thickness.
We undress in the pink room,
where the blinds are still closed.
Summer is disintegrating, the heat unravels
in the wind. I feel the skeleton inside my chest.
Outside, emaciated dogs bark in German.
The flowers fade like paintings.
Parasites chew the still water
we held our breath under.
Breeze tears through the fibers
of our bathing suits drying on the back of a chair.

City of Violent Wind

1

Heavy shutters
on the windows. A fresh nudity
in the sky, to the south, the east—

It is the wind that once threw
my high school French teacher
from her bike, headfirst into a wall.

Madame opened her eyes: a crucifix,
her two hands bandaged.

Nurses circled her bed in white habits.
Her glasses were gone.
She was American, the air smelled,
the floor was stone. She understood so little
of what the nurses said in their southern accents,
asking her
if she was hungry.

2

—I looked down and saw his hands

moving above the keys
while the arpeggios tripped over themselves (Ravel??)
six floors up from the medieval street.

Mars shone:
a bright dot.

No longer like wind, but water,
the relationship between the piano and the sound of water,
orderly,
and yet
tenuous, volatile.

We saw Lortie do it in Chicago.
All technique, no passion, a critic said, but that was what I liked.

In Avignon, I watched hands
crossing one over the other.
Then a student or girlfriend
came and sat next to him on the bench
and he kept playing.

3

The window sucking in the curtains,
the earthenware pot filled with thistles.
My T-shirt up to my chin, the wind blowing tissues from the bed—

You on your bicycle ahead of me, sweat—
The hares hid when we rode past—
Pollarded trees with gnarled stumps

which men hung their straw hats on—
The abandoned hut with the bashed-in roof
where we didn't suck each other—

The room aristocratic
but faded,
two antique twin beds pushed together.

4

The churches darkened.
The shutters latched.
The season of the end
of desire (Petrarch

met Laura here). A dog slumps
down, his owner is an old woman holding a glove
to her lips—
I imagine for a moment that the love

she gave her life to
is buried in that abbey of stone.
City of violent wind, but no wind.

Students drink by the wall,
the bars are open
and play American music.

History of Pleasure

I walked by myself to the market
past ruins with broken
bodies of stone, where even
a fragment of a man could undo me.
I bought herbs wrapped in paper.
Light shone through the glass of our apartment.
You had been showering,
the smell of mint invaded the room, your hair was wet.

Mosquitoes

The summer the elderly died
in their walk-up apartments,
I projected my homosexuality onto everyone.
The sea frilled
like expensive lettuce. The beach became crowded
with working-class people.
They sat in the dark sand, their dogs too free.
A zapper killed mosquitoes baroquely.
My teeth were yellow from coffee and wine.
Every desire I had I wanted enacted—
on the beaches, in bathrooms, in train stations.
Faded buildings with no air-conditioning, the windows open,
you couldn't drown out the noise.
When the power was cut, it was like a new artificial night on my eyes.

Sarcophagus

My grandfather burned fires when we were kids
down by the lake in a structure he made
from stacked stones, the ash
so soft and powdery, almost white.
There were burnt shards of birch
cracked and black as pieces
of a sarcophagus. You can't witness your own death,
I remember someone saying in a seminar
while we were discussing a Celan poem
in which the speaker is digging
through the ash. It was a Thursday,
I drank a bottle of mineral water with Ronald,
sun on Holbeinstraße, sun on Morgensternstraße.

Blue Anther

The forest is full of weapons like ours.
A white hind—
I guess it has pleased his Caesar to make
him free. It starts to rain. The laurel droops.
Lately, something has taken hold
of me—not hunger, not shame. It is like a flower
blooming in the injury.
Our sneakers in the doorway, our black cellphones
in our jackets on the floor.
We sleep among skins, I bleed
in your mouth. The flesh
isn't flesh
anymore. Now it can lie down.
Now it can sleep.

Weekend

I spend half the day in the bathtub, trying to read something,
trying to find something to latch on to.
I read a newish novel, very classy, winner
of the Prix Goncourt, now in English.
The water gets cold.
No real interest in the narrative. Everything's stopped. My life
in equilibrium: my love is happy, my other loves
in New York or Berlin, one in Mexico City, waiting things out;
they've forgotten about me.
I drink a can of seltzer in the tub.
Actually, there's something I like in this novel.
Something finally.
When the boys are on the beach, one of them puts his sunglasses
     inside a sneaker while he swims.

The Romans

It doesn't take long to find a new lover.
He takes a Polaroid of me on the steps
of the chapel. My eyes are full of him. My fingernails
blue from putting my hands in my jeans.
He shakes the photo with two fingers,
the sun uglies me. He leaves
it on the table of candles where others
place coins and roses. When he grabs me
by the hair and shouts into
my mouth, a pearlescent filament
is strung between his body
and mine. I wake up on a crisp afternoon in November
with things to buy:
cheese and apples, chenin blanc, flowers.

Summer and Fall

Fall I hate the most.
Fall is the season
of the end of love.
All summer, we were shirtless, we sat
in foldable chairs, drinking white wine
from plastic cups, reading sentences aloud from our magazines.
I know I shouldn't become so attached.
I'm embarrassed how much I need to hear the words.
I touch the veins
in your feet. Now I live
in a city with no seasons. My nipples are soft.
My heart the heart
of a cheating whore. Now summer
is the season of leaving.

Tiberius

I kept my bathing suit on through dinner.
After a day of nothing,
pretending to read, waiting for a man to touch me.
I lay motionless.
The electric fan making the room noisy,

                    blowing around all those drafts,
drafts in which the lover is transformed
into an animal.
           The sun got high.
Goats named after Roman emperors
ate from my hand.
               Shoeless in rows of shrubs
in an absolutist garden.
The season was ending.
I was alone. My odor was like a fern's.

The Fables

In school, we read a ridiculous story by Aesop,
one not involving wise or foolish animals or insects, but one in which
    a god allocates emotions
to the parts of the body. Intellect to the mind, Love
to the heart, etc. etc., until only the asshole is left,
to which the god assigns Shame. Understandably, Shame is unhappy
with the accommodations, but it's too late. Shame
curses, "If Eros should ever seek to occupy that place,
I will leave the body for good." This is why
homosexuals have no shame, according to Aesop,
or one of his Victorian translators. According to me, this is why
there is no moral order
to my sexual imagination, and why, praising my looks and hair
and white flesh as I lie with you, then falling
silent for days at a time, you really are the master of my pain.

Quail

He addressed me as "my quail, my sweet quail."
He was easy to obey.
It was a year ago in Connecticut, I remember the middle of his body,
the beach, a hollowed-out tree in the sand, changing leaves,
the parking lot of a senior citizens home—
When will I see him again, I asked myself
while I was with him,
taking off my socks in the sand,
and again the next day, when I wasn't,
and the day after that,
and the day I woke up
and there was snow on the tennis courts.

The Arab Baths

We removed our clothes and clung
to rough towels. There were decorative holes,
small and shapely planets
in a manageable cosmos,

through which artificial light rained down.
In the shower, touching oil to my hair,
I tried to imagine the lover as a mirror of the self,
but I was distracted by the tessellated wall of bats—

unlike us, each body cut
and polished to precisely the same shape
in a Moorish pattern.
We moved between the baths

like men moving through the stages of life.
First, suspended like babies
in the warm water, in need of one another.
Then into heat, where candles flickered on a shelf

and mint tea filled a tiny flute of glass rimmed in silver.
Standing up, you were the glistening Tree of Knowledge,
until hot mist fell against my eyes,
obscuring everything.

When we plunged into the colder waters,
we could not feel the constituent parts
of our bodies anymore,
as if death were freedom from desire.

In the steam room, on a warm marble table,
I was pre-existent, but then
the time-bound fragrances came: the air filled
with lavender, red amber, and flower of pomegranate.

Under Limestone

It rained in fluted torrents,
the earth smelled of manure.
It was like desire
entering and possessing you quietly.
We undressed.
The sun through the windows made shapes
on the couch I lay facedown on.
Our jeans were soaked
and wrinkled on the radiator, our socks heavy.
Then your eyes were opening a little.
Then you could hear the mopeds starting up again.
When it was dry enough, we found a small bistro
where we had prosecco and fries,
and took pictures of one another in our damp clothes
under trees and buildings
of the hated régime.

Things That Are Rare

It is so easy to imagine your absence.
Maybe it is night, we are still handsome.
All the young are.
It is so easy. Another thing to be beautiful.
How gently the curtain falls back down
and the room is dark again, the season
of in-betweenities,
my eyes heavy, my lips numb.
Fingerprints on the unjacketed books.
Inside the collars
of the shirts in the open closet—
An affluent night.
You've touched everything in my small room.

Beneath Our Skin

Blood just beneath our skin,
I dreamt I was on a leash
he kept yanking back . . .
In Mexico City, we saw an angry dog
on a choke chain,
partially opened roses,
alcohol over ice.
While he held me,
I woke to an obscene message from someone else.
I hardly slept, I yawned through breakfast.
I put on short shorts.
I bought
the cheapest roses and plunged them in water.

Rilke Poem

His studio like a Bohemian's but astringent,
a poem by Rilke framed beside his bed
in the kitchen, which he read to me
the night it rained hotly, in a language I used to know,
and summer curled the crisp edges
of a map taped to the wall.
I covered his eyes with my lips, but he pushed me away,
the window unit sputtering
black flecks onto the sofa, which he'd covered
with a sheet, on which we sweated
from our hair and armpits.

Looking at Medieval Art

I'm by myself again, looking at bright green tapestries,
a painted box in which was kept
a human heart. A skeleton with a long, pointed pole
piercing the ribs
of a dying man.
I lunch alone on chunks of venison. The Black Death
feels distant, like you.
The medieval streets have been widened by
modern instruments of pain.
I look for a stranger with whom
to act out the gamut of jealousy, obsession, control—
until his body, like a soul, slips out from mine.

Cypress

Dark, still pools like primitive mirrors
give us back our images. A pink
evening, sempiternal trees.
For males, the image is the essence of sex,
so we labor to perfect our physiques.
So subtle, that affect: I'm unable
to swallow my own saliva.
I think: I am pulverized. Let it be
his hand that strangles
me to death. We cum
in an unknown pre-Greek language.
Having no names to call after one another,
we expel water, hormones, and minerals from our skins,
like the cypresses.

Linen

In my room, there are flowers wrapped in newspaper.
Hotels are places of sadness.
Outside, the grass scorched by the sun,
but the pool is so cold.
It's the end of summer, but
the weather changes: another season enters it.
The monastery I visit
is where pilgrims came to see
the facecloth of Christ.
It never really wrapped his head.
Dusk comes suddenly. Gold on the edges of clouds.
In 1791, they arrested the monks and set their books on fire.
I will be young for many years.
I wear a sweater by the pool.

Mummified Bird

The Pharaoh who loved me died.

They put his body in oil and linen.

In life, he called me pretty birdy.

I pulled dead feathers from my side for him, I practiced

holding his finger. We both were chosen

from among our kind. He sent slaves

to a room they never came back from

and once a wife he didn't love. I love

the marble shape of him, packed with fragrant herbs.

Priests attended my cage, like doting women.

Then a man put his hands on my head

and I felt the air no longer. He barely touched me

I was so breakable. The cats were mute, like death.

The jackal-headed man held my heart.

Does the earth belong to him now?

If there is a soul, I don't think it can let go

of such splendor: his silent mouth,

his brain, like mine, outside of him—though he walks now

in another place, in another perfect body

with a new wife to love him.

Museum

From one room to the next, the gods
are becoming younger.

One's face is broken, but he still holds
his flute and harp. For a week, I have wanted to be broken

in your hands, offering nothing
in return. The earliest pipes made of river reeds

have disintegrated.
I worry our hearts are growing cold.

At the far end of the room,
Mercury is a boy already.

I will abandon you, I will come back.

September

The stores are closed,
but the street is busy—
All the bodies that move
hide their dead lovers.
The street name commemorates the month and day of independence,
but not the year. A wall of portraits: a fist
on the hilt of a sword, fingers
on documents
of learning and possession.
In that kingdom, I'd be killed for passive love.
We walk in the rain.
The sea so seamless.
We drink liquor in tall glasses without ice.

Bottom's Dream

The less he can see me, smell me, hear me, and taste me
the better. It's by design, Madonna
playing, my shirt open, another season entirely
outside, where we spill out onto an almost-winter street:
I remember smoke drifting from his lips
making Rococo shapes, his mouth sticky. The limestone walls
making us so hairy and dynamic
by contrast. I think of those paintings kept behind a curtain
in a perverted bishop's collection.
Don't I know then: my death will be a thin fabric
he kisses me through. Fuck. I shouldn't say that:
I'm from New Jersey, my dad was an executive, my fantasies of
    violence are trite.
Still, I thought it; everything humid
for a minute, the lindens shedding globby tears.

Opulence

The night river calms me with its slow dirty movements.
I walk home briskly, in a black baseball cap.
I work at the fringes of the day. I write poetry in bed
and criticism in the bath.
Among my friends here, I have a man
who calls me love names
in four languages. Once, in a moment, I thought I wanted to die
of his pleasure, but that was a wound
speaking. The history of this place
abounds with wounds.
Mobs of vandals have ransacked the villas.
A very rich man on his deathbed
from a corrupt family who loves the arts
was fed a medicine of powdered pearls.

You Couldn't Lose Me

It was like waking up in California—
the awkward blossoms,
the sky an aggressive blue. I remember the smell
from your armpits, the greenhouse windows covered in white paint,
where the air was heavy. The silver
weeds. A small herd
of farm animals at the Agricultural College
wore the field to dust.
The wind was hot and fresh
on our faces. The donkey looked so dumb
trying to walk. It was simple: Beneath your shirt
was skin. I remember that first year,
pulling your briefs from the hamper.

Male Beauty

I bought a bag of hard green pears today.
I came home and sat in our room
listening to music for hours,
solo piano, things from France, from the beginning
of the century.
When we were very young, your forgiveness
humiliated me. I knew
you would be asleep when I got back.
It is night outside
and raining. It is the same night
that fills the ruins.
You are naked, drowsy, lost. Stay like that.
In my favorite recordings,
you can hear the pianist breathing.

Night and Day

There's an orchid on the kitchen table.
Mapplethorpe said in flowers we can see
symbols of good and evil, but also see the masculinity
and femininity of things: a penis,
a vagina, or occasionally both. The famous statue of Night
at the Medici tombs was male, then female,
but it is sexless in the true night. One time a man
put a sleep mask on my eyes.
When I removed it, the light of day seemed to enter me
again. I bled from my mouth and rectum.
Dust encircled my face like a corona.
There are hours in this apartment
when all you see is dust,
when I pull the shades all the way down
so the Heriz won't fade.

French Novel

You were my second lover.
You had dark eyes and hair,
like a painting of a man.
We lay on our stomachs reading books in your bed.
I emailed my professor. I will be absent
from French Novel due to sickness. You put on
some piano music. Even though
it was winter, we had to keep
the window open day and night, the room was so hot, the air so dry
it made our noses bleed.
With boots we trekked through slush for a bottle of red wine
we weren't allowed to buy, our shirts unbuttoned
under our winter coats.
The French language distinguishes
between the second
of two and the second
of many. Of course
we'd have other lovers. Snow fell in our hair.
You were my second lover.
Another way of saying this:
you were the other,
not another.

Pernod

In the summer I slept without a shirt.
I dreamed light BDSM dreams.
I walked through forests of tall black trees
and maidenhair ferns. I guzzled
Pernod, I took pictures
of the carvings above the black columns
of the local chapel: a man carrying a sheep,
a miser being chastised.
To give oneself to a hundred lovers: hard.
To give oneself to one: also hard.
I watched an older man and a younger man tanning themselves
by the freezing pool.
I stayed up all night.
I cleaned my genitals in the sink.

Feast Days

1

On our drive down from Toulouse,
I practice silence. I am reading about men who strove to lose

affections. I bring a secondhand *Lives of the Saints,*
two kinds of bread, a blanket, and some paints.

It is our fifth summer together. Ahead of us, churches and red-roofed
    homes,
narrow streets, and tombs

of martyrs. Against the southern sky, the thick
octagonal dark of a tower. The roads are paved in brick.

In the Place de la République,
a pheasant shrieks, which is a kind of music.

2

The Rue St. Antonin. Nothing in the air
but leaves and heat, trembling above the square

like a broom pushing dust, then blown
back down the avenue where you and I are walking: the color of bone.

They store the relics here. Here they minted money
in medieval times. This road leads to the sea.

Here Fauré was born to schoolmasters.
Their fifth son. He learned on the harmonium. Pilasters

flank the doorway. Outside a restaurant,
we read a menu behind glass, a list of things to want.

3

The bits of hair and blackened bone traveled here
on a ship, though the exact year

is unknown. We go our separate ways.
You read a map. I am downstairs, where a shawled organist plays

one of Fauré's songs. Music out of silence.
In a window, Christ rends

a piece of bread in two. When a woman lights a candle, a shadow
    flutters
on the wall. Something echoes in the rafters—

a human voice, not yours. It isn't mine.
I move along and see the altar and the dark sealed shrine.

4

I hold yellow ochre
to the canvas. We are sitting, both of us, en plein air.

You touch my arm. I want these leaves
to be the perfect shade. My sleeves

are rolled up. The palette knife is warm. When the sun
moves, the shadows change. The one

I am holding is no longer right. I search the box of pigments
next to you. The paint stiffens

quickly. I want to remember.
I mix green and gold and umber.

5

I lift my glass to you. The wine's from nearby Aude.
A handsome waiter showed

us how to swirl it in a glass. "N'est-ce pas
que c'est bon?" It's good. A Vespa

is leaning on its kickstand. Windshields gleam
in the midday sun. Under the blue striped awning, you seem

unchanged as any papal portrait. Sometimes
on the signs and menus, they write the older names

for things. The patio, the wine, the conversation—
we're older than we were in Boston.

6

Where we run for cover, an arc of water courses
from a gargoyle's mouth. The rain forces

us under a sheltered passage. Following you, I run my hand along the
     grout
between the bricks. Water gurgles in the spout

then stops in the animal throats, where it spilled
a moment ago, waiting to be filled

again like holes left where men quarried
blocks of limestone. With ropes and wooden pulleys, they carried

them here, knowing the call they answered
was all that mattered.

7

I listen to Fauré. I read about the popes
before we fall asleep. I like to paint landscapes,

though I always see you looking. We've discussed
our differences. We both distrust

abstraction. Later, when we're tired of walking, let's stop in front
of some beautiful place and tell each other what we want.

There is so much to say. It may take until night.
We ask someone for directions. I write

them down, because I don't listen. If we reach the tower,
the scrap of paper says, we've gone too far.

ACKNOWLEDGMENTS

I am grateful to the editors of the following magazines for first publishing these poems:

The Adroit Journal: "Bottom's Dream," "Spring Wedding," "Tiberius"
The Believer: "Blue Anther"
The Common: "City of Violent Wind," "Opulence"
Critical Quarterly: "Cypress," "One Another," "September," "Street of Dyers," "Underground"
The Harvard Advocate: "Edible Flowers," "Pink Room," "Sarcophagus"
Hobart: "The Romans"
The Hopkins Review: "Feast Days"
Kenyon Review: "Linen," "Things That Are Rare"
The Literary Review: "Historic District"
Los Angeles Review of Books: "The Arab Baths"
The Massachusetts Review: "Beneath Our Skin"
The Nation: "You Couldn't Lose Me"
The New Yorker: "French Novel," "Under Limestone"
The New York Review of Books: "At the Rustic Hamlet Built in 1783 for Marie Antoinette, Last Queen of France"
Northwest Review: "Mummified Bird"
Poetry: "The Fables"
Quarterly West: "Coquelicot"
The Sewanee Review: "Male Beauty," "Museum"
The Yale Review: "German Cities," "Looking at Medieval Art," "Rilke Poem"

"Weekend" appeared as "April" in *Together in a Sudden Strangeness,* edited by Alice Quinn.

A NOTE ABOUT THE AUTHOR

Richie Hofmann is the author of *Second Empire* (2015), and his poetry has appeared recently in *The Paris Review,* *The New Yorker,* and *The Yale Review.* A recipient of both the Ruth Lilly and Wallace Stegner fellowships, he lives in Chicago.

A NOTE ON THE TYPE

This book was set in Adobe Garamond. Designed for the Adobe Corporation by Robert Slimbach, the fonts are based on types first cut by Claude Garamond (c. 1480–1561). It is to him that we owe the letter we now know as "old style."

Composed by North Market Street Graphics, Lancaster, Pennsylvania
Printed and bound by Friesens, Altona, Manitoba
Designed by Maggie Hinders